INMOST

Nightboat Books

CALLICOON, NEW YORK

JESSICA

INMOST

FISHER

WINNER OF THE 2010

NIGHTBOAT POETRY PRIZE

© 2012 by Jessica Fisher

Printed in the United States

ISBN 978-1-937658-00-7

Designed and composed by Quemadura
Text set in Perpetua and DIN Black

Cataloging-in-publication date is available
from the Library of Congress

Distributed by
University Press of New England
One Court Street
Lebanon, NH 03766
www.upne.com

Nightboat Books
Callicoon, New York
www.nightboat.org

for Sylvie & Dylan,

inmost & other—

I wake and feel the fell of dark, not day.

GERARD MANLEY HOPKINS

3

4

For *inmost*, the dictionary gives these definitions: 1. situated farthest within: the inmost recesses of the forest; 2. most intimate or secret: one's inmost thoughts. As the title of Jessica Fisher's second collection, *Inmost* strikes me as effective instruction. Indeed, reading these radiant poems, the sense of an interior is so acute that one can almost sense a natal heartbeat beneath the lines. And yet Fisher refuses to create a barricade between the intimate and the social. Instead, *Inmost* traces the ways sensation and thought bring the external world inward.

A number of the poems are meditations that examine the facets of an experience or even of a word. While I was reading "Mortar," for example, I thought first of a bombing. But the opposite is also contained in the word, since "mortar" refers both to the cement that holds a building together and to the shell that blasts it apart. Likewise, the twinned terms "*raise* or *raze*" draw our attention to the inseparability of creation and destruction, nurture and violence. I come to know something from following Fisher's train of thought. *Know*, as in *be familiar with* rather than *be knowledgeable*. And it's quietly exhilarating not to depend on exposition to know something.

I love the objective exploration, the juxtaposition of various denotations, but what is most thrilling is that everything simultaneously radiates connotation. In Fisher's work, the more subjective response often comes across as personal mythology. This is nowhere more true than in the long poem "Winter," which uses narrative elements to explore an intimate experience. Winter is, of course, the season in Greek mythology when daughter and mother are forcibly separated; this poem also draws upon Shakespeare's *The Winter's Tale*, in which a daughter suffers her mother's absence. Rather than create a conventional narrative, here the allusions to Shakespeare combine with seemingly personal details to form a new version of an age-old tale. The poem's fragmented style requires constantly moving inward. Pain and urgency are kept alive in this meditation, even as the poet seeks to come to terms with what is most intimate and secret.

Both "Winter" and the book's title poem, which places the reader in the midst of "the birth of the inmost," explore the mirrored relation between mother and daughter as the daughter herself becomes a mother. This productive ambiguity operates on the personal level much as do the linguistic ambiguities of "Mortar." In these psychologically sophisticated pieces, the myth that the mother is a promise kept to the child becomes a compromise for the speaker, and the promise of compromise becomes the real tale.

KIMIKO HAHN

INMOST

Hurt

Things that can't be held, can't be helped, in the mind. The latest horror of the latest war, never on these shores. Like the book of bodies you opened in a shop and then closed, choosing not to carry such a thing home. But I am guilty of false logic. Upon waking, for example, the child cries with the sound that means hurt. Dream has hurt her, I conclude, though I don't remember if there's a chapter on the infant. The dreamlife of angels is said to be made of ice and snow, white on white as if an understudy. That blankness becomes a wall of light, a screen. Or the partition your fingertips trace, passing by. Touch is a kind of love, but there's something unseen on the opposite side. Sound passes through the blockade. What to make of what you hear. "Sounds Like" a strategy in the game of charades, indicated by a hand cupping an ear. The words remain unsaid. Talk is in the head when shushing a child, when washing whites as the child sleeps, or whitewashing the walls. This is what is meant by "to draw a blank." She is practicing erasure, she is practiced at it. Turn the dial: they're turning to the war. Stitched, like a slip, on a bias. It gives a sense of the body underneath.

Day 1,715

takes the sky by force
the radio readers warming up

war an ugly word
the terminal *r*

whipped me into shape
when I couldn't say it

gagging on the
hunched tongue

they have to say it
hunker down

men in fatigues
tired of watching

the punctual day
burning through

bunk a bed
left for the watch

a cigarette
smoked down

you take a loss
it takes a lot

Mortar

Small wound toward sleep.

On the clothesline, a shirt hung by the waist, pink and white.

In the foreground, a pointing finger, the icon for *here*.

A muted keening, or rather the keening muted.

Let's make a happy mouth, she says, pretending to fuss.

It's the way she plays baby.

What comes after N?

An exclamation or a sigh, a sound that extends infinitely.

And little arms. *Why, why, why, why, why?*

Preparing the house, the body.

Like the house, stripped down.

To raze, from the French "to shave (a person, a part of the body)."

To clean, up or out.

The eyes open as if watching.

Little windows cut in the walls.

We say *mortar* both for the shell and for what it struck, *brick*
& or *stone* & .

To build or to destroy, *raise* or *raze*.

Derive

Canker in the mouth on the rose in the bole of the tree

The skin of the roof of the mouth peeling away

Vulnerable to damage, as when the name of a color and the name of a thing are the same

Bole for bole, for example

This is the color children choose for trees

Named for the thing, or the thing for the color, only most are a lighter brown

Or *bole* a clod, therefore *its* color

Fallow the color of fallow fields

Whose sheaf of wheat, whose heavy millstone sunken

Who pricketh his blind hors over the falwes

Early words, harrowed by the plow

And *harrow* for the soldiers' formation, the birds' migration

The name of their kind derived from the Greek for *wine-blossom*

Because they land there when the grapes flower

And also for the fallows they fly from, as in fallow-chat, -finch, -smich, -smiter

Names for a bird named for an ear of wheat

Or *wheatear* for "white arse"

Like driving the wrong way down the narrow highway

We saw the red car headed into trouble, the snowy mountain that rose from the desert

Danger was part of its beauty

The thin throat of the pale girl, the pale throat of the thin one

A causeway of veins running blue under her skin

The five points of the star pendant were razor sharp; one pricked the hollow and blood made a jewel there

As when the lacemaker pricks her finger: a drop of red in the
field of white

A flower named for that, at its center the bloodmark

Where desire mars the beloved, *not so white as* but *white as
can be*

Listen

I said clatter me catch me it's time I said few a fever it is time
write it are you a medium are you mark the page a conflagra-
tion can't you a burning sheet a shroud you can't see sound it
makes make it up to me if I a conspiracy if I a condition some-
thing nameless a little nauseous under the weather whither it
blows sky full lightning what does it show tangle of branches
drawn out of night a cage for the mind and then it goes dark
the eye a storm the raged wheel turning someone riding shot-
gun someone writing start at the end won't you it only gets
better voices in the backseat what is going on listen up it's hard
times listen in

Ravage

Day I wanted to break
Broken heel in the lot
A lot

& for what reason

Sun caught in the wire it was
tangled & heartfelt
it was nothing I couldn't

be or break

■

To the child learning her letters
each word stands for something
What do you stand for?

a fighting question

V for Violin, W for Walrus
or Violence & War—
we are after all to teach them

how to survive in this world

how "to continue to live after
the death of another"

■

Thought I could live in it
& not let it in, impervious as
a body floating in saltwater

eyes open to the shifting sky

Mugged with the baby
on her first birthday
& running for cover

on hot mid-afternoons

when the pop-pop or the
rat-a-tat-tat-a-tat couldn't
be passed off as fireworks—

soundtrack to the good life

lived far from war—
late-summer nights lit
by helicopter searchlight

the block blockaded—

funny where words come from
how their meanings divert
in some dark cul-de-sac—

our French brushed off so the kids

won't know what's going on
but we don't have the words for it
& *police* is the same either way—

■

Child please know
the eye is a weapon
we are heavily armed

Say what you see

Avenger or Caliber
in the vicinity
How to teach fear

& not be afraid

my charge, Duck
Duck Goose or
duck & cover

■

What they don't know
won't hurt them
the harmless world stripped

from the children's dictionary

an alphabet of loss
apricot bramble clover doe
BlackBerry for *blackberry*—

"there's only so much

their little hands can hold"
the editors explain;
the book had grown heavy

with the weight of each name—

still "apricot trees exist,
apricot trees exist"
& the bramble of blackberries

sweet in the hot sun

& the bed of clover
where the doe beds down—

■

K for King or Kosmos
why couldn't it be
the child's story

in which I was queen

The princess
granted a wish
wanted a baby

& here she said he is

Tired not sleeping
her story went on
I couldn't rightly follow

I was shaping the nipple

Hostages to fortune
their little legs entwined
Something will hurt them

This the moral of the story

2

Pare

Cliff where the cradle uncradles.
Black wings of what bird?

Black feathers of that wing.
Oh darkening!

The nail losing its edge, the apple its skin.
A paring, thrown out or off.

Here: semilune puncture.
                    Punctum: *here.*

Indent, or an indentation proving ripeness.
Bite, or a bit of light, tartsweet.

Not enough to see by.
And the jagged mountains named for teeth.

And the unnamed valley deep in shadow.
Night draped on the fields of mustard.

And a crevice, to scale or scaled.

Undone, the arrest of rest—the river.

Apparent: the sliver another sign for moon.

Moon could grow and be the moon I crave, a ripe thing:

Fathom

What if morning is not diurnal
                the sun nowhere the sea
        like two notes played over again
                until thought is a crewless boat unthinking
the little heart an impossible thing
                nevertheless marked by a sign
        the dark sky over
              below the deep sea
medium for the sound of singing
                someone knocking and already
        a you I could address dear sir
              the pleasure of your presence
already a strand upon which
                in the dark night to write
        or what does the moon contain
              that it pulls the water thus toward form

Firebird

From silence to the silenced bow, an interstitial stitch. We held our clapping hands until the tendons were the struts of wings, the fingers feather bones, and off they flew. Dart and shimmer, the lark.

Vane, rachis, calamus. Parts for the whole, as if one could make a living thing. And I did. Starch and water give a little shape. Wing on high, bird on the wind, a god there——or, *for God*, the windhover,

as in a book I read, the girl swinging higher as the swallows dipped and turned through the barn; or as, in a foreign town named for a local river, we watched the birds become bats as the world we had come to know faded to black,

yet still we knew, in that moonless night, that it had just been day, just as the television screen would give us away: at its center, a star of static, and the glass still hot——

he would press his hand to it when he walked in the door and would know, the way I knew fever when I first felt it, her brow like a hotplate beneath my palm, even her bare feet hot, no longer my body, and no longer hers—

but what takes the body as its own gives us *body*, firebird danc-
ing the fever out against the white bedsheets, a first bright
mark on that stretched and gessoed canvas—

Figure

We made a letter where we lay down, a script or scripted in
this love that we follow, this figure on ground,

& noun became verb in that grounded figure, in an arc where
we arched like bentwood or sugar

falling in skeins from the end of a spoon, the burning, cloy-
ing, flung far from the body,

until at last we had made the nest I had dreamt of, in the dream
where I knit the nettles together:

you held, in your hands, the impossible thing, the riddle that
tells of the birth of the mother—

it was fragile as snowfall and a bed for the fallen,

for the egg that you found beneath the tree where I'd found
you, the chalk blue shell of the fledgling that fell,

and I wondered then at your vestigial wings, that had borne
you up sure as I bore you:

what breaks is not broken but learning to sing——brittle as the
sugar we spun in our dancing——

of the world that might be, spinning beneath us, asleep on the
bed on the head of a pin——

Inmost

And then we were in the privacy of intimacy: from the Latin, *inmost*. With the birth of the inmost. Where we lay. Or sat, hunched in the croup tent, the kettle boiling. Hearsay, because memory is a latecomer, and because it dismembers, misremembers.

Though never "cow-heavy and floral." Nor "red and purple flowers on a black ground." An embroidered blouse, a bad perm. Or, sometime before, a photograph shows her squinting in the patch of sun, the shadow-wedge falling behind her, and then the shadows of trees. She can't, it seems, quite tell where to put her hands; her wrists crook in toward phantom pockets. A girlish figure. In the shadow, she seems handled. Someone could tell the time of day from its length. The year from the girls there, standing between her and the photographer.

Then "many bright colours; many distinct sounds." Poppies, pansies, snapdragons, strawberries. We sat in the patch, looking for red. A woman who eased herself into the pool. Who had a song for each element.

Eventually, if the mother's maiden name has fallen out of use, it becomes the answer to the secret question. The daughter's name, a password that husband and wife share. If their intimacy fails, she becomes a kind of currency, is traded. Not for goods, but seasonally. The photographs of before are a kind of contraband.

Seven years a tithe. With her gone, I dismembered the songs, *tetra coo coo coo* sung by the ailing dove. Or her voice shook itself free of its body, rode the wires. I became interested in transport. How to be in the same place at the same time. We read together, apart. The page a *Ganzfeld*. And made a home of the mind.

Because she was missing, I found her everywhere. Or "motherhood is the *fantasy* . . . of a lost territory." A *mise en abîme*. And the mother a mirror. Russian dolls in a Chinese box.

And then the smallest doll opened. She was there to hear the first cry. "One does not give birth in pain, one gives birth to pain. . . . Obviously you may close your eyes, cover up your ears, teach courses, run errands, tidy up the house. . . ." But when the inmost moves out, the body hollows—

an echo chamber. Ours is a scripted love. We stick to it. But wordless, the *shshsh* kept up long after the child's asleep. Whose lulling.

Want

As she nurses, my nipple takes on the color of her lips. This is the definition of love: to become indistinguishable. She was me, then mine; now wherever I go she follows. But which "e" is lost when *where* and *ever* meet? We went looking, though we knew we wouldn't find it. High & Low a fool's game. The contraction came into play because we need less than is sometimes given; it's a gesture to try to make what's written match what's said. They started at two minutes apart. *What's your date of birth* became a confusing question, as did the verb *deliver*. Did I, or was I? She was born of our love, to which we signed our names. A wanted child, crying *I want you* in the night. *Then want must be your master.* Hidden in the annals, the etymologist found, is another meaning, now housed in the English Dialect Dictionary. A want furrows. Why outfox it? Condensation on the window or in the mind indicates you're not where you thought. He was very handsome and had a bricklayer's hands, though he worked in concrete. He explained the logic of the contraction joint as we waited for the bus: you have to build in a break, because it grows.

Red

Wanting red, I chose rust, the nail
      an instrument of my desire, the color
         it gave the color of blood, dried—
            the adjective modifying the noun
         as color adds to the scene the exact tone,
      as if to say *It's over* or *The worst is over*,
the storm abating and the shutters

            open. He took a bone from her body
         and stitched her back closed, lay her
      in the starched bed as he burnished it bright,
lay it beside her so that when she awoke
      she found herself spooning herself,
         but still it was missing from her,
            the wound a mouth in the night,

a breach or a hunger, it was hard to say.
      Unable to choose, I made a painting
         that showed it both ways: a red field,
            like burning chaff seen at sunset,
         the fire held in by the frame—roads
      on either side of it too wide to cross,
and so I stood at the border

saying I could feel the heat of it,
though outside snow fell, and the edge
of the canvas was nothing more than
the place where the sightlines, having
crossed, fell away. That's how the end
was decided: because we were ready
for it, the story having gone on

long past where it seemed like a fable,
and because the woman's dream,
spoken aloud, had come to seem our own:
a vision she called Memory, of hair,
of eyes, of wings, fleeting, in what future
or beginning of the past outstretching,
whatever it was, we had seen it—

3

Familiar

Coming home in a city, the key stuck in a familiar way. Rattled by the thought of an intruder, *impending* a black word in the skyless night. The high pitch of the child's voice playing baby, the siren meaning we warned you, ricin found in a motel. There's never enough lead time. Spooning milk from a bowl, mommy the moon, the crust of the bread abandoned. An American child: she pulls herself up by my boots, asks to ride. Shards of the shattered plate mimicking the kernels of rice. I eat gingerly. Thoughts of returning home, years after the rented house was let go. Let go of me, she said, I want to do it myself, and climbed into your arms. How to love what leaves, how to leave your love, the cherry blossoms, plum blossoms, raining down. Language estranged in the usual ways, *quotidian* from *quoted*. It leaves a funny taste in your mouth. Now I need a red kiss, she says, and gives me her lips.

Remove

Child crying in the book, or
atmosphere another name for

mirror placed in a corner,
face angled downward

as if to pity the drowned,
bird with a broken, doll

that has fallen, *poor baby*
poor baby—
                    your words

in her mouth, *my* words
I mean, already she's bound

to my particular form of
failure, to feel for the unreal—

she was singing to her doll,
happy for the fiction,

she was the fiction of happiness
or was a doll I made, carried,

sang to of the steel flea, stolen
from the circus, of the deathbed

turned into a throne, strange basket
in which we ride, riding home.

Winter

Almost the age I
Fell from the window
The earth a home
The homeless autumn its
Fairness its gorgeous rattling

Leave-taking a compound
Thing a fracture not
Anticipated like fever at
Midnight like blood or
Bruise beneath the lobe

If idyllic the oak
Branching to the kingdom
If overcome the rheumatic
King and his donkey
Riding homeward the dove

In the nighttime garden
In the starry water
Unearthed the forgotten sound
A ringing bell like
Death on foreign sands

Where was she when
Blood bloomed its star-
Shaped banner when dark
Fell on the wakeful
Children what the answer

To the fitful question
Why ask it so
Fretfully every other car
Carries a baby that's
Why she was tired

O and drove away
Far from dishes rashes
Flew with her lover
To the foreign shore
Ate and drank elsewhere

Its azure sea or
Swept the strand with
A dove's wing how
Else to imagine the
Mother elsewhere just stop

Beneath me the baby
Busied with car keys
My daughter the age
When I when she
O what use why

■

I fell from the
Window that is to
Say I was inside

Then, not

What else to say
No not a door
Not a path leading

■

Firstfruits of your body
Wilting flower what will
Or heed the warning
Of the sailors drifting
On the sunlit sea

Their sails slack their
Faces burned the wax
In their ears foreknowledge
Of harm they know
The body is made

To suffer the children
Are made of it
From *ferre* to bear
The unwieldy weight that
Goes before you a

Cargo or stowaway these
Nine changes of the
Watery star your body
Chartered to no one
Belonging and so when

You leave the dark

Room you are not

Really to go this

Is a leaving remnant

Or scent a remembrancer—

■

O but we lucked
Out you never could
Guess how the turning
Leaves turn to hear
The homeless sound of

A voice no body
What else is lyric
But a dismembering of
The beloved it takes
Time it gives back

One at a time
Veined hands the soft
Breast your erstwhile pillow
Blazon of lips eyes
Is this what you

Wanted the mother made
Cunningly of matter an
Automaton wind her she'll
Sing O a sad
Tale's best for winter

Via

A month or a region, something you pass through. The roads on either side impassable, otherwise of course one would have chosen an alternate route.

Blood courses through the veins, feeds the heart that goes un-fed. Blue script that the nail traces in wonder, as if it answered the question, What is it you want?

Volition a bird, a kite. What hovers.

I built it of paper, then lit a match to watch it burn. The wind was high and lifted it from me: it hovered there in the home-less above, dashed down, tattered and falling, before the ris-ing air rose up again and—*oh my chevalier!*

Words are not in the body. Words move through it, lift it like a stringless kite. How do you feel? How do you feel?

In the middle of it, in the very center, at the midpoint, halfway. Foreign words on a foreign tongue.

Bildungsroman

Have you watched the bird
                the Renaissance called *windfucker*
        beating its wings to keep still?
                  That's what it was like

I looked down from above
                at the landmarked earth
        as the bird flies a way of saying
                  it's harder by foot

But the sky is also a medium
                though not like the page
        dimensional, deep
                  a different kind of sea

■

Body says open, open
        we could go down here or here
    follow the lead
        of the unafraid eye

My mind protected me
        from the flip side of joy
    it was a sort of a glass
        I stayed warm inside

A nondescript place
        blank as a safehouse
    I took down a book
        to pass by the time

■

The book is a kind of body
    turns out that is so
  book cracked open
     the sensual world in code

It was bedtime or naptime
    when mind took off in me
  as proof of thought
     was a little engine whirring

I had to think hard
    to keep out of harm
  the trees and powerlines
     a net of obstruction

■

The way forward like following
        a chalkline in the snowfield
    day measured by the progress
        of the shadow on the wall

I should say of the sickroom
        though I was in body whole
    a meetinghouse whiteness
        but how to know if spirit moved

The frozen stream another surface
        for snow's accumulation
    the mind like that also
        slowly moving underneath

Ride

Scratch of the pencil means we're not in the book means the book is closed there's no point to the cover it covers over in stultifying snow it asks you to be or to have been a nothing buried somewhere the mark that marked you a wish for somewhere new to go if you had a car or a girl a bike a plow any other mode of transport bend and you'll be ridden a helper or heaped upon each child clambering for position every other word a pornographic what something not written the action offstage they've been doing it for a while I've done it before I can show you see I can show you what might come of it pen on paper or what mark what might something takes the mind for a ride shake the cramp it's time to go now it's time

4

Spell

Find my eyes, I tell her as she buries her egg in my nest. At its center is the yolk, which sees or seems like the seeing part of the eye. Afraid I wouldn't be able to spell it, I wrote it on my hand, alongside "yoke," the silent *l* not to be confused with the silent *e*. "Yoked by violence together" creates of the prepositional phrase "by violence" a structure like the yoke itself, which makes of two beasts one will. He could equally well have written "Yoked together by violence" and it would and wouldn't have been the same. What to do when one won't follow, the plow stuck at the end of the row or her eyes still open, the driver or mother growing impatient. A hand held over her eyes as if a hood, *Close your eyes* a lullaby or a command. *Should we fight over sleep?* a ridiculous question, like asking *How's it going?* of the man who can move only, who can only move, who only can move one eye. Not for lack of trying. Language fails to capture the severity of the situation in which he found himself, his body unyoked from his mind. He was taught to write by closing his eye. "The weight of the world is on our shoulders; its vision is through our eyes; if we blink or look aside . . . we inflict on the world the injury of some obliquity." Caught in the act, "red-handed" though the ink was blue, I confessed to taking from my hand what I should have known by heart. And although all these words are in fact stolen, and mean more and less than I intend, when he opened my palm and read what was written, I felt ashamed, and lowered my eyes—

Refract

What do you have to do today or what do you have to do with day

The sun an eye in the mind's eye

Immanent or emanant

Early studies on vision thought it was a kind of light, the rays of sight reaching out from the eye, the fire inside it very hot some days

They must have gone mad trying to see themselves see

It is a problem of materiality, like that of the icecap, the hushed voice saying *ne touche pas* or *only with thine eyes*

Trying to hold a friend's eye as she speaks of the small room they shared, the bed doubling as a table

But the passing cars flash their moving image, are mirrored in the glassed-in café alcove

So that the car that just passed out of sight returns there, driving the wrong way down the busy street

Its image collides with the actual cars, they cancel one another out

There is a science for this, light caught in or on the surface of things, things made of light

The woman in the Whitney, for example, leaning up against a wall that wasn't there

The artist sued for making nothing

But light *is*: there is a name for each kind of reflection

Iceblink, watersky

They went looking for what they'd seen, a glimmering island in the eye only, the sea-ice breaking behind them

Caught off guard, as when the moving sidewalk comes to an end

I was looking up at the cranes painted on the plate-glass window, the white of their bodies running past the limits of their bodies, thinking of materiality, of outline

It is after all a fiction we follow, the mind working overtime

They made it back to camp finally but remained mistrustful of the ice, mistrustful of the eye

Though they've been dead a long time, still you can see them there in the found footage

The winter ice holding for now, a hole carved in it

The Inuit woman beats her sticks together first as if fishing, then as if dancing

You have to infer her song

I reached my hand into the dust-riddled light, the beam she rode breaking around me

And I was for a moment not a body so much as a screen

And she was light, was nothing, was dancing

Vigil

Again the stag
walks by with the thrust thrust

looks back, two pointer
That's one way to mark time

■

Was a male word once
vigil of *vigilante*

The Night Watch or
posted at the barricades

■

Nine birds on the bush
Who knows how many in it

Across the estuary
a town with a few lights on

The egret in the fields between
also a kind of light

Takes flight over them
Alights further on

■

What can no longer be seen
still is sometimes

either way it crosses into memory
as if the darkness

which is almost here
disassembled the world

■

Stillness of the black
screen of night

lit here and here
like gunfire

a word chosen to say
even here we are at war

which is unrevoked
a red-lined word

■

World we live in
we don't know what it means

we watch over it
can't see much now

■

Water in the narrow canal
catches whatever light is left

is a silver shadow
a sliver through dark fields

It points to the lights
a car if moving

if not, someone lives there
is there now

or leaves the light on
to keep watch

Blackwater

screen going dark
another kind of metaphor

to be at a loss
and to remain there

opposed to illumination
night at home here

the screen a mirror
for the dark night

"above the law"
a prepositional nightmare

what segues from war
interest at the expense

the immense loss

■

obscurity untwines
an unbroken line

I wanted to put right
the evanescent beyond

forgive the author
who follows after

for whatever is gone
she has painted a sign

Elegy

To see in the dark   Or stitch a blind seam

As if piecing together   The patchwork of forest

But I can't see she said   Where did the sun go

I think how I might show her   My little Galileo

A paper mâché cosmos   Orbit and rotation

All along we knew   We were also moving

In the drunken night   We lay on the cold earth

Waiting for disaster   The word of course meaning

Stars falling from the sky   Floater on the eye

As if a sunspot   A slow obliteration

Of embryonic origin   Who are you they asked

What do you see   If not the boundless sky

To answer you spoke   Of the eye's particular static

Familiar and degenerate   But there is a world unseen

Green beyond green   Cloud cover as though

A form of sleep   In the quiet room

Several of us wept   When he said elegy

The parade of image   On the whitewashed wall

Marking pre- and post-   Idyllic

Or was it only Eden after   And obliteration a foil

As night for starlight   I bore her in winter

The green returning   Tongues of the dead

Licking the hillside   I bore her in wartime

The radio pretuned   News of destruction

Coming over the airwaves   What was is no longer

The fieldnotes record   In Thoreau's Walden

Rose lilac and buttercup   Gone from the woods

Or what is untimely   Narcissi in winter

What were we thinking   When we weren't thinking

The moon clear at midday   But I'm not ready for night

What does it stand for   Fear of the dark

The skeletal shape   Of the world we knew

A carcass of sorts   I see with eyes closed

Or is death the mother   As Stevens wrote

After

Fluent silence
the black and white
type a winter

scene type of
winter
sight-line or

through-line
the snow-lined
tableau half

paralyzed—
an old man
making a scene

■

You were with him in the attic room
There are always two shut in together
Turning the pages of the opened book

What he saw, you saw
Through the magnifying lens

■

under	sun	over
and	a	and
over	sky	under
the	burns	the
black	in	wind
bird	his	goes
flies	eyes	too

■

Now the grass, tomorrow
the profound change—
contagious, the stark dignity—

Taken

This

      grasping,

  in   silence of

    thy days   thy dreaming nights

■

                              if it

        haunt   and chill
                          thine own
    So
        thou be conscience

■

would

thou wouldst

again

be   calmed—

■

red life

—see here it is—

I hold it towards you.

Derive: The italicized line is from Geoffrey Chaucer's *The Canterbury Tales*, and the poem's final line quotes William Carlos Williams' "Queen-Anne's Lace."

Ravage: The revisions referenced are to the 2007 edition of the *Oxford Junior Dictionary*. The line "apricot trees exist, apricot trees exist" is from Inger Christensen's *alphabet*.

Firebird alludes to Gerard Manley Hopkins' "The Windhover."

Figure references, in its final line, George Oppen's poem "The Little Pin: Fragment."

Inmost: The first quote is from Sylvia Plath's poem "Morning Song," the second and third are from Virginia Woolf's autobiographical "A Sketch of the Past," and the final two are from Julia Kristeva's essay "Stabat Mater."

Winter borrows its title and several lines from William Shakespeare's *The Winter's Tale*.

Via is indebted to Gerard Manley Hopkins' "The Windhover" and to Caroline Bergvall's sound-work "Via: 48 Dante Variations," which compiles the translations into English of Dante's opening lines:

> Nel mezzo del cammin di nostra vita
> mi ritrovai per una selva oscura,
> che la diritta via era smarrita.

Ride was composed while listening to Caroline Bergvall's recording of her poem by the same title.

Spell: Samuel Johnson complained that the metaphysical poets' work consisted of "heterogeneous ideas . . . yoked by violence together." The quoted line is from Virginia Woolf's *The Waves*.

Blackwater: "To be at a loss and to remain there" is a rephrasing of a line from Michael Palmer's "Notes for Echo Lake 3."

The fourth section of *After* reorders parts of William Carlos Williams' poem "Spring and All."

Taken selects words from an untitled poem John Keats wrote in the margins of the manuscript of "The Cap and Bells." The poem reads in its entirety:

> This living hand, now warm and capable
> Of earnest grasping, would, if it were cold
> And in the icy silence of the tomb,
> So haunt thy days and chill thy dreaming nights
> That thou wouldst wish thine own heart dry of blood
> So in my veins red life might stream again,
> And thou be conscience-calmed—see here it is—
> I hold it towards you.

∎

Grateful acknowledgment to the UC Berkeley English Department for making the writing of this book possible through a Holloway Poetry Fellowship, and to the editors and staff of *American Poetry Review*, *Puerto del Sol*, and *Women Studies Quarterly*, where some of these poems first appeared.

Thanks to Kimiko Hahn, Stephen Motika, and Nightboat Books for supporting this project, and to Quemadura for the design.

Love and gratitude to my first readers, Julie Carr and Margaret Ronda, for your friendship and inspiration; to my mother, Ann Fisher-Wirth, for bringing me to poetry; and to Dan Clowes for making a life with me.

Nightboat Books, a nonprofit organization, seeks to develop audiences for writers whose work resists convention and transcends boundaries. We publish books rich with poignancy, intelligence, and risk. Please visit our website, www.nightboat.org, to learn about our titles and how you can support our future publications.

This book was made possible by a grant from the Topanga Fund, which is dedicated to promoting the arts and literature of California.

The following individuals have supported the publication of this book. We thank them for their generosity and commitment to the mission of Nightboat Books:

KAZIM ALI

ANONYMOUS

ELIZABETH MOTIKA

BENJAMIN TAYLOR

This book has been made possible, in part, by a grant from the New York State Council on the Arts Literature Program.

State of the Arts

NYSCA